Hop, Ski

Count!

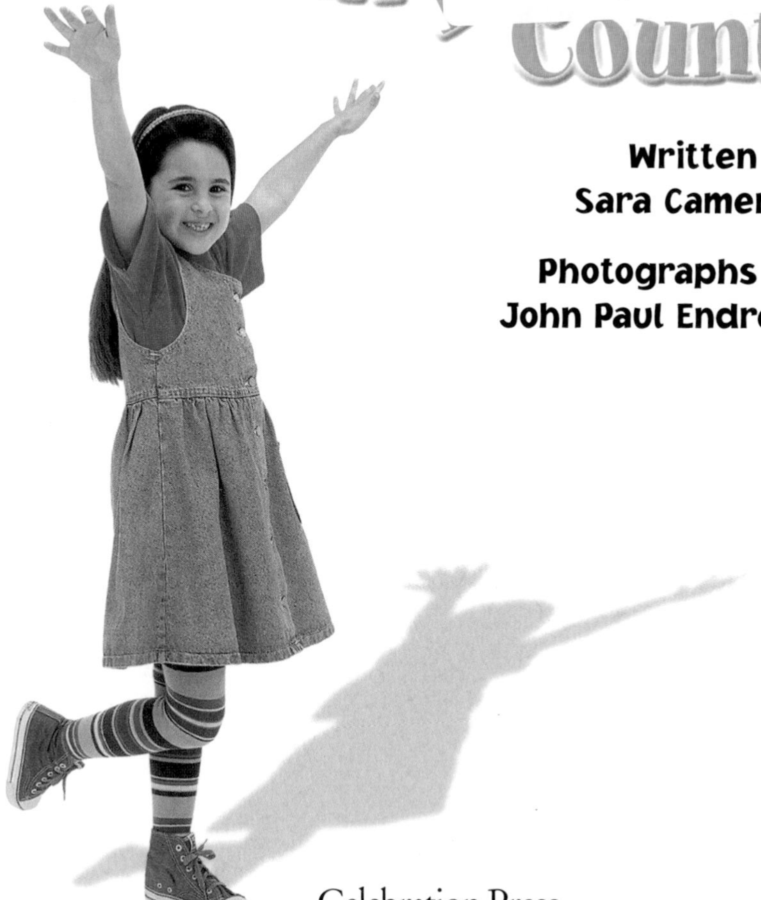

Written by
Sara Cameron

Photographs by
John Paul Endress

Celebration Press
Parsippany, New Jersey

How many noses?
Each child has one nose.
You can count them like this:

1, 2, 3, 4, 5, 6, 7, 8, 9, 10 noses.
That's called counting by ones.

How many legs?
Each child has two legs.
You can count them by ones,
or you can count them like this:

2, 4, 6, 8, 10, 12, 14, 16, 18, 20 legs.
That's called skip counting
by twos.

How many crayons?
Each child has three crayons.
You can count them by ones,
or you can count them like this:

3, 6, 9, 12, 15, 18, 21, 24, 27, 30
crayons.
That's called skip counting
by threes.

How many fingers?
Each child is holding up 5 fingers.
You can count them by ones, or you can count them like this:

5, 10, 15, 20, 25, 30, 35, 40, 45, 50 fingers.
That's called skip counting by fives.

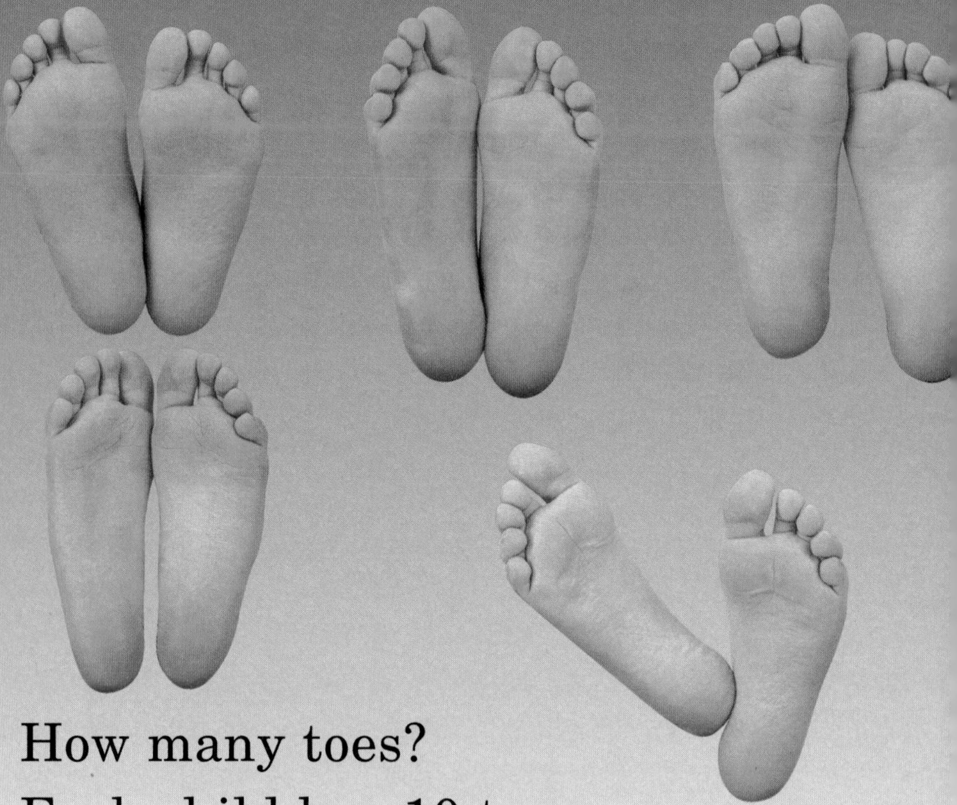

How many toes?
Each child has 10 toes.
You can count them by ones,
or you can count them like this:

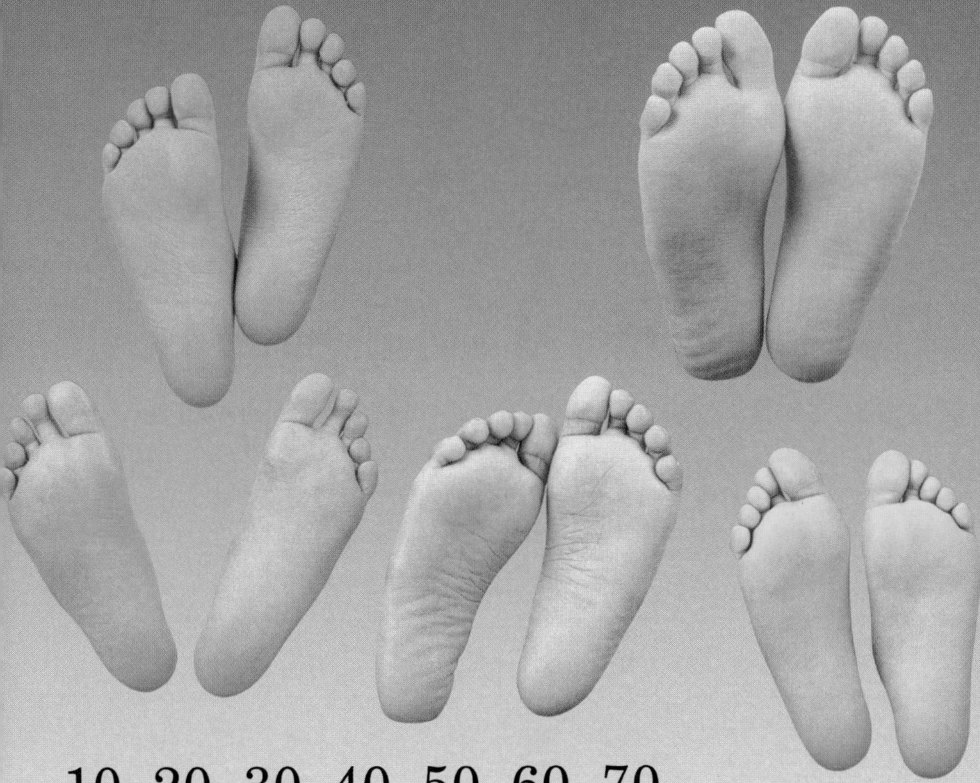

10, 20, 30, 40, 50, 60, 70,
80, 90, 100 toes.
That's called skip counting by tens.
Skip counting makes counting
things faster and easier.

1	2	3	4	5		7	8	9	10
11	12	13	14	15	16	17	18	19	20
21	22	23	24	25	26	27	28	29	30
31	32	33	34	35	36	37	38	39	40
41	42	43	44	45	46	47	48	49	50
51	52	53	54	55	56	57	58	59	60
61	62	63	64	65	66	67	68	69	70
71	72	73	74	75	76	77	78	79	80
81	82	83	84	85	86	87	88	89	90
91	92	93	94	95	96	97	98	99	100

Look at the hundreds chart. It can help with skip counting. Try some skip-counting hopscotch.

To skip count by twos, the girl hops into or shades every other number box in the grid.

1	2	3	4	5	6	7	8	9	10
11	12	13	14	15	16	17	18	19	20
21	22	23	24	25	26	27	28	29	30
31	32	33	34	35	36	[illegible]	38	39	40
41	42	43	44	45	46	[illegible]	48	49	50
51	52	53	54	55	56	57	58	59	60
61	62	63	64	65	66	67	68	69	70
71	72	73	74	75	76	77	78	79	80
81	82	83	84	85	86	87	88	89	90
91	92	93	94	95	96	97	98	99	100

To skip count by threes, the girl hops into or shades every third number box in the grid.

1	2	3	4	5	6	7	8	9	10
11	12	13	14	15	16	17	18	19	20
21	22	23	24	25	26	27	28	29	30
31	32	33	34	[illegible]	36	37	38	39	40
41	42	43	44	[illegible]	46	47	48	49	50
51	52	53	54	[illegible]	56	57	58	59	60
61	62	63	64	65	66	67	68	69	70
71	72	73	74	75	76	77	78	79	80
81	82	83	84	85	86	87	88	89	90
91	92	93	94	95	96	97	98	99	100

To skip count by fives, the girl hops into or shades every fifth number box on the grid.

How could she use the grid to count by tens?

1	2	3	4	5	6	7	8	9	10
11	12	13	14	15	16	17	18	19	20
21	22	23	24	25	26	27	28	29	30
31	32	33	34	35	36	37	38	39	40
41	42	43	44	45	46	47	48	49	50
51	52	53	54	55	56	57	58	59	60
61	62	63	64	65	66	67	68	69	70
71	72	73	74	75	76	77	78	79	80
81	82	83	84	85	86	87	88	89	90
91	92	93	94	95	96	97	98	99	100